JURGEN

Borgo Press Dramas by FRANK J. MORLOCK

Chuzzlewit
Crime and Punishment
Falstaff (with William Shakespeare, John Dennis, and William Kendrick)
Fathers and Sons
The Idiot
Jurgen
Justine
Lord Jim
Notes from the Underground
Oblomov
Outrageous Women: Lady Macbeth and Other French Plays (editor and translator)
Peter and Alexis
The Princess Casamassima
A Raw Youth
The Stendhal Hamlet Scenarios and Other Shakespearean Shorts from the French (editor and translator)

JURGEN
A PLAY IN THREE ACTS

FRANK J. MORLOCK

Based on the Novel by James Branch Cabell

THE BORGO PRESS
MMXII

JURGEN

Copyright © 1980, 2012 by Frank J. Morlock

FIRST BORGO PRESS EDITION

Published by Wildside Press LLC

www.wildsidebooks.com

DEDICATION

*For Gerry Tetrault, Dana Woloshen,
Ernest Ibarra, and Carmen Martínez*

CONTENTS

CAST OF CHARACTERS 9
PROLOGUE 11
ACT I, Scene 1 17
ACT I, Scene 2 37
ACT I, Scene 3 49
ACT I, Scene 4 59
ACT I, Scene 5 63
ACT II, Scene 6 69
ACT II, Scene 7 87
ACT II, Scene 8 107
ACT III, Scene 9 121
ACT III, Scene 10 149
ACT III, Scene 11 155
ACT III, Scene 12 163
ABOUT THE AUTHOR 185

CAST OF CHARACTERS

Jurgen

Monk

Old Monk

Neighbor

Dorothy la Désirée

Hetman Michael

Guenevere

Knight

Lisa

King Gogyrvan

Merlin

Brown Man

Anaitis

Hooded Man

Chloris

Priest

Queen Dolores

Devil

Second Devil

Coth

Satan

Florimel

Young Jurgen

God

Koschei

Other Priests

PROLOGUE

A roadway in a medieval setting. A monk with a sack enters and falls over a rock. Jurgen, a merchant in his early forties, enters from the opposite direction.

Monk

Owww!

Jurgen

Are you all right, brother?

Monk

May the devil who placed this cursed stone in my way kiss my arse!

Jurgen

Fie, brother! Has not the devil enough to bear as it is?

Monk

It hurt my big toe confoundedly. Damn the devil to

Hell, I say.

Jurgen

It does not behoove God-fearing persons to speak so ill, and with such disrespect of the divinely appointed Prince of Darkness. Consider this monarch's industry! Day and night he toils at the task Heaven set for him—placing temptations in our way, so that by avoiding them, we may reach our salvation. And with such consummate skill and professionalism. Why, but for him, you, a monk, and I, a pawnbroker—would be penniless. And think of all the other professionals that would starve—lawyers, pimps, prostitutes. Why our whole economy would be disrupted.

Monk

Stuff and nonsense. Fuck the devil and all his works.

(Exit monk with his sack.)

Jurgen

No doubt your notions are pious—but mine are more practical.

(Enter an old monk of very kindly mien.)

Old Monk

Thank you, Jurgen, for your good words.

Jurgen

Who are you? And why do you thank me?

Old Monk

My name is no great matter. But you have a pure heart, Jurgen. May your life be free from care.

Jurgen

I am already married.

Old Monk

What? How dreadful. Such a fine clever poet like you.

Jurgen

Haven't written a line—not one—since the honeymoon.

Old Monk

Ah, I suppose your wife's opinion about poetry does—

Jurgen

—Does not bear repetition, at least in polite company. I am sure you are unaccustomed to such language.

Old Monk

I fear Dame Lisa does not understand you, Jurgen.

Jurgen (astounded)

Sir, how is it you read a man's most private thoughts?

Old Monk

It's a knack I have. Tsk, tsk. This is most deplorable. Most deplorable. The first person to speak well of me in centuries—well, well, say no more—such a person deserves a reward. Good day, Jurgen. You will have your wish. And not just one.

(Exit Old Monk.)

Jurgen

Good day to you, sir. Nice, well-behaved gentleman, that.

(Enter a neighbor.)

Jurgen

Good day, neighbor.

Neighbor

Jurgen, Jurgen. Your wife has been carried off by a

devil and disappeared in a cloud of smoke.

Jurgen

Really? When?

Neighbor

Just now. This very moment.

Jurgen

Well, well. A wise man always speaks well of everyone. In a cloud of smoke, you say?

Neighbor

The devil himself carried her off. Better come at once.

Jurgen

I suppose I should go to make sure. But I have confidence in Lisa. She can take care of herself in any company. In a cloud of smoke. Fancy that! Well, it will be quiet at home for a change. Though I may have to cook my own supper, I fancy I shall digest it better.

Neighbor

Come along.

CURTAIN

ACT I
SCENE 1

In the Garden of Youth. A beautiful garden. Several young lovers in medieval dress. Dorothy la Désirée, a beautiful girl of sixteen, is wandering by herself and meets Jurgen, who enters dressed in a beautiful shirt.

Dorothy

Why have you come to this garden, stranger?

Jurgen

Well, because I am looking for my wife whom I suspect was carried off by some poor devil.

Dorothy (archly)

You are glad to be rid of her, are you not?

Jurgen

I confess a certain—relief.

Dorothy

Then why are you here?

Jurgen

Because everyone said it was the manly thing to do, to try and find her. I have always been too deferential to the opinion of mankind.

Dorothy

How did you get here?

Jurgen

You wouldn't believe me. You are a monstrously clever person.

Dorothy

Try me.

Jurgen

A centaur that I met on the road brought me. He gave me this shirt.

Dorothy

That's ridiculous. I don't believe you.

Jurgen

Perfectly all right. You'd be daft if you did. But are you not Dorothy la Désirée—the only woman I ever loved?

Dorothy

Certainly, I am she. Count Emmerich's daughter.

Jurgen (bitterly)

And the wife of Hetman Michael.

Dorothy

That oaf! I would never marry him.

Jurgen

So you told me when I was young. But you married him all the same.

Dorothy

You're funny. Are you mad? Who are you, friend, that you have such curious notions about me?

Jurgen

I will answer that question, even though you clearly know the answer. I am Jurgen.

Dorothy

I know but one Jurgen—and he is much younger than you.

Jurgen

Ah, I understand. I have returned to my youth. I have heard of this other Jurgen. A monstrously clever fellow—and he loved you.

Dorothy

No more than I love him. A whole summer I have loved him.

Jurgen

The poor devil loved you, too. I can testify to it. For a whole summer and perhaps all of his life.

Dorothy

You talk in riddles, friend.

Jurgen

That is customary when age talks to youth. For I am a man of forty, and you—you will be sixteen in two months—for it is August—the August of a year I had not expected ever to see again.

Dorothy

You really are a strange fellow—but I like you. In fact, I liked you instantly, as soon as you told me your name was Jurgen.

Jurgen

Well—and what can I do about it? Somehow, I—who am but the shadow of what I was, walk with the love of my youth. In this same garden, there was once a boy who loved a girl with such a love as it puzzles me to think of now. And for a whole summer these two were as brave and comely and clean a pair of sweethearts as the world has known.

Dorothy

Tell me about yourself, sir. For I love all tales of lovers.

Jurgen

Ah, dear child—if only I could. Who can tell the glory of a first love—moonlight nights—unreasonable laughter—and the feeling that suddenly you are—alive. A story not worth raking up at this late date. Preposterous, really.

Dorothy

What happened then?

Jurgen

There was a difficulty. She was a count's daughter and he was the son of a pawnbroker.

Dorothy (excited)

I know a case just like it. (curious) What happened?

Jurgen

Well—it seemed a transient discrepancy because our hero intended to become an Emperor.

Dorothy

And then? And then?

Jurgen

Well—our hero had to go away for a while—and before long he learned that his lady had married Hetman Michael.

Dorothy

Isn't that strange? There is a Hetman Michael that my family is plaguing me to marry. But I won't. (thoughtfully) Anyway, go on.

Jurgen

There's nothing further to tell, really. The boy became a pawnbroker and married a shrew—and suffered ever after until a devil befriended him and carried off his wife.

Dorothy (disappointed)

So his life was ruined!

Jurgen

To be perfectly honest, no more than most. He met her again in her married state and decided she was rather dull and stupid—yet—well—he could not retain his composure in her presence.

Dorothy (interested)

So he still loved her!

Jurgen

My child, you are incurably romantic. He hated her—naturally.

Dorothy (bawling)

Oh—couldn't they have become lovers?

Jurgen

No, it did not work out. She took many lovers—and he, the legend tells, had many affaires de coeur—but never did these two become lovers.

Dorothy

What an awful, cynical, stupid story. I am going to leave you.

Jurgen (quickly)

No. Now that I have found you again it would not be possible to lose you. Not so long as there is Justice upon Earth. Why, there is no imaginable God who would permit a boy to be robbed of so noble a dream twice.

Dorothy

You—upset me. It seems to me you are my Jurgen—yet you are not my Jurgen.

Jurgen

But truly, I am Jurgen, and I have won back that first love whom every man must lose no matter whom he marries. Had I known you awaited me in this garden of youth—between dawn and sunrise—I would have had the heart to live. Surely, you are a reparation. I will not let you go—for you and you alone are my heart's desire.

Dorothy

Hands off, old lecher! I can't stand an old man!

(Jurgen is pushed off balance and she escapes.)

Jurgen

Well, I am answered—yet, I know it is not the final answer. Am I so changed?

(Enter Old Monk.)

Old Monk

Good and evil keep exact accounts, and the face of every man is their ledger.

Jurgen

What is Dorothy doing here?

Old Monk

Why, all women a man has ever loved live here—for very obvious reasons.

Jurgen

That is a hard saying, friend. This is a world that never was. Was Dorothy la Désirée an imaginary creature?

Old Monk

Poet! Do you not know she was your masterpiece? Actually, she was a shallow little bitch with passable looks and a bad temper—consider what a goddess you made from such material.

Jurgen

Who can be proud of such folly? Yet—who can regret it? My heart will keep the memory of that bliss until life ends.

Old Monk

There is something in that, Jurgen.

Jurgen

What is the good of revisiting one's youth if one is no longer young?

Old Monk

Do you think that will help?

Jurgen

It can't hurt.

Old Monk

So be it. All who see you now will see you to be Jurgen as you were twenty years ago. Only your mirror will tell you the truth.

Jurgen

How can I thank you?

Old Monk

It is my pleasure. I like experiments.

(The Old Monk exits.)

Jurgen

Well, it's certainly nice to be young again. Now, where did he go? Oh, well. Hmm, my shadow certainly isn't that of a young man. Let's hope no one notices. Look at these doomed people. There is my mother Azra—she never had any confidence in me—the only woman, I suspect who really understood me. She will die in ten years—and I won't learn of it for several months. Ah, but these things are not yet—and besides, these things are inevitable. Why think about it. Yet the inevitability of all this is decidedly not fair. And there is Rainault Vinsauf laughing. In six years he will have his throat cut like a pig while held by three Burgundians. I wonder if he would laugh quite so loudly now if he knew that. And I shall forget all about him, although he is worth three of me. How can they laugh? Still, they may be wise in not glooming over what is inevitable; and I certainly cannot go so far as to say they are wrong—but still—at the same time—

(Enter Dorothy. She runs to him.)

Dorothy

There you are. I met the most horrible man.

Jurgen

My heart's desire, I am sad tonight, for I am thinking of what life will do to us, and what offal the years will make of you and me.

Dorothy

Sweetheart, do we not know you are to be an Emperor and conquer the Holy Land?

Jurgen

We are more now than we will ever be. Our splendor will be wasted. And such wastage is not fair.

Dorothy

First, you will conquer France; then you will preach a Crusade and lead an army against the infidels.

Jurgen

No, heart's desire—I shall be quite otherwise.

Dorothy

How proud I shall be of you.

Jurgen

You will not think of me at all.

Dorothy

Can you really think I care a damn for any man but you?

(Hetman Michael approaches.)

Dorothy

I have promised to dance with this old fart, and so I must. He must be nearly thirty.

Jurgen

Now, by Heaven, wherever Hetman Michael does his dancing, it will not be hereabouts.

Michael (very civilly)

I fear I must rob you of this fair lady, Master Jurgen.

Jurgen

The next dance is to be mine.

Michael (good-naturedly)

We must leave it to the lady.

Jurgen

Au contraire. Were I to do that, my fate would be sealed. I am not the same callow thing I was twenty years ago.

Michael (puzzled)

Your remarks, Master Jurgen, are somewhat strange.

Jurgen

But, I will tell you a stranger thing. There seem to be three of us here, but actually there are four.

Michael

Four?

Jurgen

The fourth is a goddess whom no prayers or sacrifice can placate.

Michael

You speak of death?

Jurgen

You have a jumping wit, Hetman. But hardly quick enough to outrun the whim of the Goddess.

Michael

Ah, my young bantam—the Goddess and I are acquainted—I have dispatched many stout warriors to serve her underground.

Jurgen

My notion is, Hetman, that the Goddess should not leave us unescorted. One of us, as a gentleman, cannot fail to accompany her.

Michael

You are insane. But you extend an invitation I cannot possibly refuse.

Jurgen

Hetman, I bear you no ill will. But it is highly necessary that you die tonight in order that my soul not perish twenty years hence.

(They draw their swords and fight. Hetman is easily Jurgen's master.)

Jurgen

This is highly annoying, Hetman. You are the better swordsman and it is not fair.

Michael (disarming Jurgen)

So now, Master Jurgen—there is the end of your nonsense. But you needn't wet your pants—I don't intend to kill you—it is not my custom to kill children—and besides, I prefer to dance with this lady.

(Michael turns his back to Jurgen and offers Dorothy his arm.)

Jurgen

Not this I call insufferable! Did I come back to my youth only to lost it again? This is unjust.

(Jurgen snatches a dagger and stabs Hetman Michael in the back.)

Michael

Oh, I am slain. (dies)

Dorothy

Oh, dear, dear. But I don't blame you—he was such an old fart and he was going to carry me off. I'll bet he was over thirty. (thinking seriously) But, what will become of you? They'll hang you for sure.

Jurgen

I will take my doom—and without whimpers, so that I get justice. But I shall certainly insist upon Justice. The man was stronger than I and wanted what I wanted. It wasn't fair. So—I have compromised with necessity to get that which was requisite to me. I cry for Justice to the power that gave him strength and gave me weakness—but gave us both the same desires. (impressively) I have done what I have done.

Dorothy

Oh, my hero. You're so brave.

Jurgen (dragging the body and concealing it under a bench)

Rest here, brave sir, until they find you.

Jurgen

Come to me now, heart's desire. Here I sit, (Dorothy sits on his lap) with my true love—upon the body of my enemy. Justice is satisfied. Oh, that I could detain this moment! Could I but get into words the softness of this girl's hair—for I shall forget all this beauty—this be-drenching moonlight.

Dorothy

You shouldn't have done it. Even if he was an old fart—he wasn't so bad.

Jurgen

Whatever the future holds for us—and whatever the happiness we two may know—we shall find no moment happier than this.

Dorothy

Poor, dear, brave Jurgen. You did all this for me, But, what will become of you?

Jurgen

Who knows? But I am wiser now than then. So I will not waste the one real passion I have known—nor leave unfed the one desire of my life—nor live to regret I did not avail myself of your love before it was taken from me. Remove your clothes.

Dorothy

Here—over a dead body! Are you mad? What kind of a girl do you think I am, anyway? And I thought I could trust you. Somebody may come at any moment.

Jurgen

Then, we have no time to lose.

Dorothy

Let's go to my room.

(Jurgen and Dorothy hurry off, eager for the game; a bell tolls.)

CURTAIN

ACT I
SCENE 2

A cavern. Guenevere lies asleep under a canopy. Jurgen enters and doesn't see the enchanted Princess at first.

Jurgen

Well, well, it's true that enjoyment spoils things—but this is unheard of. How did I get in this cave? One minute with Dorothy and the next in the middle of nowhere. What's this? (seeing Guenevere) Well, well, this lady has certainly been enchanted. Now, there are certain orthodoxies to be observed in waking an enchanted Princess—and I may consider myself at liberty to observe them since my wife is nowhere in the neighborhood. Of that I am tolerably certain, for I hear no talking. Therefore it is only fair to kiss this Princess. Justice demands it.

(Without more ado Jurgen gives Guenevere a passionate kiss.)

Guenevere (returning the kiss)

I knew you would come.

Jurgen

Did you? I didn't. But, (kissing her again) I am very glad I came.

Guenevere (disengaging after a while)

Time passes, we must fly.

Jurgen

Well, but is there not time for a little fun? For I would deal fairly with you.

Guenevere

The others are waking, too. Life is very contagious.

Jurgen

Upon my word, this is a delightful place to be leaving.

Guenevere

I am Princess Guenevere—daughter of Gogyrvan, King of Gladthion and the Red Islands.

Jurgen

I am the Duke of Logreus. (aside) It would be unjust for a pawnbroker to rescue a Princess. At any rate, not if he would deal fairly with her.

Guenevere

The troll King Thragnar is responsible for this enchantment.

Jurgen

That ugly fellow I saw as I entered?

Guenevere

We must make a sign of the Cross. He beholds and trembles.

Jurgen

I now regret that I flung away a cross in this neighborhood very recently—I trust the action was understood. If Dorothy had not insisted, I would never have thought of doing such a thing. I intended no reflection upon anybody. I hear him coming this way—Thragnar will be at hand presently.

Guenevere

Even so—he can do no harm unless we accept a gift

from him.

Jurgen

Then, why worry?

Guenevere

The difficulty is that he will come in disguise.

Jurgen

Why, the solution is to accept gifts from no one.

Guenevere

How clever you are. Also, there is a sign by which you can know him. If you deny what he says, he will always concede you are right.

Jurgen

What an inhuman trait! He ought to be very easy to distinguish.

(Enter a knight in black.)

Knight

Sir Knight, you must yield me that lady.

Jurgen

I would not go so far as to contradict you, but I think you are mistaken.

(They fight and the black knight is easily killed.)

Jurgen

Do you think that this is Thragnar?

Guenevere

There is no possible way of telling. Yet, he offered nothing—and you did not quite contradict him, so he didn't agree with you—so that proves nothing—which is what I just said.

Jurgen

Let's have a look at him.

Guenevere

But that will prove nothing. He is always in disguise.

Jurgen

Such sartorial habits introduce an element of uncertainty. In justice to ourselves we will just keep on the safe said. (running the knight through again)

Guenevere

You think of everything. That's what I like about you.

Jurgen

Assuredly, a magic sword is a fine thing, and very necessary equipment for a knight errant of my advanced age.

Guenevere

Do not talk that way. You are not so old. My husband-to-be, King Arthur of the Britons is over ninety years old.

Jurgen

You are a Princess of both beauty and discrimination. What, after all—is forty-two, if one is well preserved? Uncommonly intelligent lass—reminds me a little of Dorothy. I like this Princess—in fact, I adore this Princess.

(Enter a woman of about thirty-five carrying a vase.)

Lisa

Oh, my dear Jurgen—how fine you look. I have been with a dark gentleman who is a great friend of yours. (softly) You must be very tired, darling. You and the young lady must have a sip of this and then I'll tell you what happened to me since I was carried off.

Jurgen

It's a long while since I saw you in such an amiable mood, Lisa, my love.

Lisa (smiling)

I have learned to appreciate you since we separated.

Jurgen

No doubt it took the fiend himself that took you to bring about that wonder! You see me with a woman and you haven't scratched either of us. (astounded) Why, you haven't even raised your voice or let out the teeniest little curse! Where is your jealousy now that there is reason for it? No, this is a miracle beyond the power of any fiend.

Lisa

Ah, I've done a lot of thinking, Jurgen dear. It seems to me you were right most of the time.

Guenevere

Did you note that? What woman ever admits that to her husband? Surely, this is Thragnar in disguise.

Jurgen

In all events it is surely not the woman I married. Lisa—

Lisa, dear—I am through with you. You tire me. You talk too much—no woman is your equal in volume or continuity of speech—but—you say nothing I have not heard seven hundred and eighty times at least.

Lisa

You are perfectly right, my dear. But then I never pretended to be as clever as you.

Guenevere

You see, you see! She cannot contradict you, as any woman would. It is Thragnar.

Jurgen

Certainly, it is not a woman. (to Lisa) Spare me your beguilements. Besides, I am in love with this Princess. I know what you would say—spare me your recriminations. If you had stayed the merry girl I married, I would love you still—but you elected to become a plain, meddlesome and short-tempered old shrew.

Lisa

You are perfectly right—from your point of view. But, how could I help getting older—and it made me so mad, you see.

Guenevere

Old hag! She must be at least thirty-five, if she's a day.

Jurgen

This is an astonishingly inadequate impersonation, Thragnar—as any married man will tell you. Any remaining claims you have on me, I regard as manifestly unfair. No alimony. I won't pay a cent. What's more, I pledge my undying love to this lady—who is—and this will break your heart—the fairest lady I have ever seen.

Guenevere (simpering)

And besides that, I'm young.

Lisa

You are right. I am entirely to blame. But you will never understand the feelings of a wife. Here is our wedding ring then, Jurgen. I give you back your freedom. And I pray that this Princess will make you very happy, my dear. Happier than I made you. For surely you deserve a Princess if any man ever did. (sobbing, she offers the ring)

Jurgen

It is astounding that a demon of your renowned talents should prove so incompetent an impersonator,

Thragnar. It raises the staggering proposition that most married women must go to Heaven—a thought not to be entertained by any married man. I am sorry, I can't take the ring. I am not accepting gifts from anyone today. But you understand, I trust, that I am hopelessly enamored of the Princess on account of her matchless beauty?

Lisa

I cannot blame you, dear. She is the loveliest person I have ever seen.

Jurgen

Hah, Thragnar! I have you now. A woman might just possibly admit her own lack of beauty; but no woman that ever breathed would admit her rival had a rag of good looks, no—not even if she looked like Queen Helen herself.

(Jurgen runs Lisa through.)

Guenevere (jumping up and down, applauding)

Well done! Bravely done! Now the enchantment is dissolved forever. (leaping on his neck) My clever hero. My matchless champion.

Jurgen (a little uneasy)

I wish there were some surer sign of that. Shouldn't

there be a clap of thunder or something—and other customary phenomena? Nothing is changed except that the woman who was talking to me now lies at my feet—in what must be admitted is a very untidy condition. It annoys me that Thragnar omitted no detail—not even her crooked little finger. Such painstaking attention to detail worries me, for you conceive, Madame, I should not like to make an error in this matter.

Guenevere

You think too much, darling. Thragnar or not—in any event she was a witch.

Jurgen

Well, in any event, I only tried to do Justice.

Guenevere

Think no more of it. Come, we must go to my father for your reward.

CURTAIN

ACT I
SCENE 3

Somewhere in the King's palace. Enter King Gogyrvan, Guenevere's father and Jurgen.

Gogyrvan

Demand of me what you will, Duke of Logreus—and it is yours for the asking.

Jurgen

Sir, a service rendered so gladly should be its own reward.

Gogyrvan

I am quite of your opinion.

Jurgen

Therefore, restore to me Princess Guenevere in honorable marriage—as I am but a poor forlorn widower. I love your daughter with my whole heart.

Gogyrvan

What has the condition of your heart to do with such an unreasonable request? My daughter is pledged to Arthur, King of the Britons. If I were to break the promise, it would mean war—and thank you—I don't care to fight with that formidable gentleman.

Jurgen (despondent)

Then I must lose Guenevere forever?

Gogyrvan

Did I say that? I merely said Guenevere must marry this Arthur. His ambassadors, Merlin—a terrible magician—and a witch called the Lady of the Lake will be here soon to fetch her. In two months. Meanwhile, you two have youth—and love—for playthings.

Jurgen

Heartless old man—how can I be happy when I must lose her forever?

Gogyrvan

You say that because you think it is expected of you—and because you had too much wine last night. Would I be insane enough to marry my daughter to a mere duke? First, you would tire of her. Granted, she is nice-looking—because she takes after my side of the family—but, between you and me—she's a terrible flirt and not terribly bright. Second, if you disappoint me, and don't tire of her—she will presently tire of you. Frankly, she's just like her mother—and I assure you, the apple hasn't fallen far from the tree—she will always be making eyes at some man or other.

Jurgen

I had noticed that trait already.

Gogyrvan

Good! You're not as besotted as I thought. This Arthur is going to have his hands full. She'll be making it with every knight at his roundtable. Not to mention the grooms.

Jurgen

That is a melancholy prospect.

Gogyrvan

Meanwhile, I do not deny your rights as the champion who rescued her. No one—least of all me—will criticize you or her—if you make the most of that turn.

Jurgen

You are a bit liberal in your attitudes towards these things.

Gogyrvan

If you get smart with me, sonny, I'll lock you both up in separate dungeons till the wedding day. But it strikes me that you should be the last to grumble.

Jurgen

But critical persons will say that you are taking small care of your daughter's honor.

Gogyrvan

Well—as to that—though my daughter has always been a quiet little minx—I never heard that Thragnar was anything of the sort.

Jurgen

Whatever are you hinting?

Gogyrvan

My dear duke. My daughter has been a captive, held in a cave by a Troll King for several months—and things happen in dark places like caves even when there is no Troll King present. My job is to marry my daughter and to ask no unnecessary questions. I rejoice in her rescue. Such discoveries as may be made by her husband are his concern—not mine. And I trust her to prevent that sort of thing. Besides, a woman's honor is concerned with one thing only—and it is a thing with which the honor of a man is not concerned at all.

Jurgen

Your aphorisms are abominable.

Gogyrvan

Give thanks that you were born a man—and in all matters that concern my daughter, I would have you lie like a gentleman.

Jurgen

Sir, you are a person of somewhat degraded ideals.

Gogyrvan

Remember, I regard my daughter with considerable affection—if you should ever be tempted to become candid.

Jurgen (horrified)

But, with the Princess, sire, it is unthinkable that I should not deal fairly. I would only do simple justice to her.

Gogyrvan

See that you do. And now—be off with you.

Jurgen

One question. Do you think this is reputable conduct in a King?

Gogyrvan

Hardly. It is philanthropy. Good-day.

(Gogyrvan leaves.)

Jurgen

Well—I intend the girl no harm. Perhaps what is about to happen will broaden her ideas—make her more sophisticated—it's been known to make a woman more attractive. Yes, I shall deal fairly with her—but let us have a little honest rapture and excitement over this highly promising situation—is there no heart in this spry young body you have regained?

BLACKOUT

When the lights go up, Jurgen and Guenevere enter in whispered conversation.

Guenevere

I would never consider such a thing—and whatever must you think of me to make such a proposal! (primly) Besides, I have no idea what you are talking about.

Jurgen

It is a matter which can only be explained in private.

Guenevere

If I were to report your insolence to my father—

Jurgen

You would annoy him exceedingly—

Guenevere

He can be a mean old fart at times.

Jurgen

My love is worship and no less. And you have no faith in me!

Guenevere

Very well. I trust you.

Jurgen

Now, swear solemnly to trust me forever in everything.

Guenevere

Well, just this once. I swear. Shall I send for a priest?

Jurgen

My dear, there is no need to trouble a priest about our private affairs.

Guenevere

Now I regret that I made so solemn an oath. Your trick was unfair!

Jurgen

Has anyone ever accused Jurgen of being unfair? That's my line. Fear not. I will deal fairly with you.

Guenevere

Ah, but you know that you are doing wrong. (loosening her dress)

Jurgen (innocently, while assisting her expertly)

I, doing wrong! I, who am simply doing my best to entertain you.

Guenevere (still removing her clothing) You know very well what I mean!

Jurgen (still assisting expertly)

But, I protest—I have not the least notion. How can I know what you mean, when you refuse to tell me what you mean? You should have your seamstress make a little change here—it will make things easier.

Guenevere

How stupid of you it is to sit there grinning in a way that makes me blush. It's because nobody ever told me about these things.

(Guenevere is now totally naked.)

Jurgen

Yet, I dare say Thragnar—the Troll King being very wise, must have made zoology and biology much clearer—

Guenevere

Thragnar was a skilled enchanter, (demurely) and through the potency of his abominable arts, I can remember nothing about Thragnar. (wrapping herself expertly about Jurgen)

CURTAIN

ACT I
SCENE 4

Merlin's rooms at Gogyrvan's palace. Merlin is casting a spell when Jurgen enters.

Jurgen

You wished to see me, Merlin Ambrosius?

Merlin

The King is sending Guenevere to Arthur accompanied by one hundred knights. As evidence of his deplorable sense of humor he has numbered you among the knights.

Jurgen

That man is neglecting his duties as a father, and that is not fair.

Merlin

Now it is rumored that you and the Princess are given

to conversing a great deal in private—and Arthur has never approved of—garrulity, shall we say. For you to come with us to Camelot would be highly inconvenient—and decidedly dangerous.

Jurgen

Not only that—it would ruin what would otherwise be a perfect memory.

Merlin

You are well advised. Put Guenevere out of your head—for in your heart, I think she never was. (showing a crystal ball) Look here.

Jurgen (peering in)

This is horribly embarrassing. I am not used to being seen in such unclad condition or in such indecent postures.

Merlin

What you see, Duke Logreus, has been seen by me.

Jurgen

Well, if I did that sort of thing, I believe I would blush.

Merlin

Look again.

Jurgen (gasping)

Who's this fellow? How dare he touch the Princess in such an indecent manner?

Merlin

He is called Lancelot du Lac.

Jurgen

I will challenge him this instant! Why, that two timing—

Merlin (cutting him off)

It has yet to happen—but it is inevitable.

Jurgen

Nothing! Suppose I kill him?

Merlin

You cannot. It is fate.

Jurgen

Well, well, I see the Princess will speedily console

herself in my absence. Hmm. She never did that with me. Does Arthur know this?

Merlin

He was forewarned—but it was useless. His doom was written before he was born. What must happen will always happen. Foreknowledge is not prevention.

Jurgen

Still—I shall find it hard to forget the Princess.

Merlin

If you would forget her—take this token to the Druid forest. There you will meet a brown man who will put Guenevere out of your mind.

Jurgen

What one needs at a time like this is a kind friend. I'll do it.

CURTAIN

ACT I
SCENE 5

The Druid forest. Jurgen enters with the token Merlin gave him.

Jurgen

Brrr! It will be amusing to see what comes of this business—not that I believe for a moment in such nonsense. Still, it is unjust to deny nonsense a fair trial.

(A brown man dressed in a monk's habit enters. He is playing on a reed pipe.)

Jurgen (showing the token)

Praise be to you, Lord of the Two Truths. I have come to thee to learn thy secret. I would know thee for what thou art.

Brown Man

I am everything that was and that is to be. No man has been able to discover what I am. (examining the token)

Merlin dared not to come himself because Merlin is wise.

Jurgen

What are you about to show me?

Brown Man

The nothingness that is everything.

(Jurgen stares as if hypnotized, then struggles to free himself from the trance.)

Jurgen (screaming)

It is not true. What you have shown me is nonsense. It is sorcery—and abominable blasphemy. In a word, it is something I do not choose to believe.

Brown Man (smiling)

Even so, you do believe me.

Jurgen

You ought to be ashamed of yourself.

Brown Man

Merlin would have died without regret to see what I have shown you. No other mortal has seen it.

Jurgen

Why, if there is a bit of truth in your silly puppetry, this world is but a bubble—a bubble which contains the sun and the moon and the blue stars—and still is but a bubble. I must cleanse my mind of this foulness. You would have me believe that men, all men who have ever or shall ever live, are of no importance. That even I am of no importance!

Brown Man

Wisdom like that vexes you—doesn't it?

Jurgen

Why, there would be no justice in such an arrangement. No justice at all.

Brown Man

It vexes even me at times—but it is Koschei's will.

Jurgen

Who is Koschei?

Brown Man

He who made things as they are.

Jurgen

Never heard of him.

Brown Man

He never heard of you either.

Jurgen

It is too terrible to be believed.

Brown Man

How if I killed you now—I being what I am! Make answer, you who chatter about Justice.

Jurgen

You can kill me—but it is beyond your power to make me believe that I am unimportant. I will not believe in the insignificance of Jurgen.

Brown Man

Fool! Have you not just seen what you never can forget?

Jurgen

I think, therefore—I am. I am—therefore I refuse to believe I ever will not be. I am—if nothing else, a monstrous clever fellow—and somehow I will contrive a trick to cheat oblivion when the need arises. Of course, you may be right, and certainly, I cannot go so far as to say you are wrong—but still—at the same time—

Brown Man

Before a fool's opinion of himself, even the gods are powerless—and envious, too.

CURTAIN

ACT II
SCENE 6

Jurgen is at a window in the castle of King Gogyrvan. He is watching the departure of Guenevere.

Jurgen

Farewell, Queen of my heart.

(Trumpets sound. A beautiful woman approaches.)

Anaitis

Arthur will have a beautiful Queen.

Jurgen

Yes. He is greatly to be envied. But, why do you not ride with them, as you were an ambassador like Merlin?

Anaitis

My part was ended when I introduced the young Queen to my nephew, Lancelot du Lac.

Jurgen

Is it true you reared him at the bottom of a lake?

Anaitis

Yes, it is true.

Jurgen

A rather odd way to be reared, I should think. Must have been a strange childhood.

Anaitis

He has grown to be an upstanding knight. He will do me great credit. By now Guenevere agrees with me. And so, my part is done and I am off.

Jurgen

Back to your lake?

Anaitis

No. I am off for Cockaigne.

Jurgen

And what is this Cockaigne?

Anaitis

It is an island where I rule.

Jurgen

I had always heard you referred to as the Lady of the Lake. I always fancied you at the bottom of your pool. I didn't realize you were a Queen, Madame.

Anaitis

Why, there are many things unknown to you in this uncertain world. Man has nothing except his own body—and yet it is capable of much curious pleasure.

Jurgen

I believe you speak wisely.

Anaitis

All in Cockaigne are wise; for that is our religion. But what are you thinking, Duke of Logreus?

Jurgen

That your eyes are unlike the eyes of any other woman that I have ever seen.

Anaitis

Why, then you must come with me to Cockaigne and see if you cannot discover wherein lies that difference. For it is not a matter I would care to leave unsettled.

Jurgen

Well, that seems only just to you. Yes, I certainly must deal fairly with you.

(The scenery changes. Erotic sculptures descend and the window disappears, to be replaced by torrid vistas of tropical skies.)

Jurgen

Now certainly, Queen Anaitis, you have an unusual taste in sculpture. I think that fellow there is carrying things to extremes. (pointing to a Hindu god in rapture)

Anaitis

Well, we have arrived safely.

Jurgen

It was curious.

Anaitis

What was?

Jurgen

The crew of your ship.

Anaitis

What of them?

Jurgen

I never saw any of them.

Anaitis

They are well-disciplined mariners.

Jurgen

Not a one. I could hear them though. Sounded like bats chirping. They are hardly common seamen.

Anaitis

They are outlanders and speak a language of their own.

Jurgen

Hum! Perhaps we should now turn to the pursuit of those curious pleasures which you were telling of.

Anaitis

I am very willing—but there is a ceremony to perform.

Jurgen

What is this ceremony?

Anaitis

It is called the breaking of the veil.

Jurgen

I will taste any drink once.

(Anaitis claps her hands. A hooded man with a lance enters.)

Hooded Man

Behold the lance which must serve you in this adventure.

Jurgen (taking the lance)

I accept the adventure because I believe the weapon to be trustworthy.

Hooded Man

So be it! But, as you are, so once was I.

Jurgen

I wonder what he means by that?

(Jurgen takes the lance and shakes it. The tip is red with blood.)

Jurgen

I am a man born of woman. Behold! I am found worthy to create that which I may not comprehend.

Anaitis

May your strength be as the flame of the sun. (kneeling, she touches the erect lance lovingly) By the power of the lifted lance.

Hooded Man

So be it.

Jurgen

I upraise you above all things.

Anaitis

When the lance is lifted, I speak with the tongue of every woman and my eyes shine with the eyes of every woman, I who am daughter to the sun.

Jurgen (muttering)

This is confusing. I thought she was a lake goddess or something.

Anaitis

I, who am all pleasure, all ruin, and a drunkenness of the senses—I desire you.

Jurgen (holding the lance erect)

There comes no other god where I am. My will is justice.

Hooded Man

So be it! But, as you are, so once was I.

Jurgen (under his breath)

Now what does he mean anyway? (resting the tip of the lance in Anaitis' hands) I am life and the giver of life. Open, therefore, the way of creation. For that is the law. That is justice.

Anaitis

In Cockaigne there is no law save—Do that which seems good to you.—

Hooded Man

The ceremony is ended.

(The Hooded Man turns on his heel and exits.)

Jurgen

I wish that fellow had stayed. I wanted to have a word with him. Well, well, these mummeries are a little old-fashioned. Still, woman must be humored.

Anaitis

I am a mystery. A mystery of nature.

Jurgen

No matter what you are, my dear—I am sure that presently you will tell me all about it. I know you will deal fairly with me.

Anaitis

I shall do what becomes me, Duke Jurgen.

Jurgen

Precisely, my dear. Be true to yourself whatever happens. Now, I have noticed that every woman is most true to herself in the dark.

Anaitis (twining around him)

That, I'll prove.

QUICK BLACKOUT

Cockaigne, the Palace of Anaitis. When the lights go up, Jurgen and Anaitis enter in conversation.

Jurgen

You mean to say that silly ceremony was a marriage ceremony?

Anaitis

Certainly, my dear. I am a very respectable woman.

Jurgen

Well, never did a monstrously clever fellow marry a high Queen with less premeditation.

Anaitis (soothingly)

You were controlled by the finger of fate.

Jurgen

That makes one seem rather trivial.

Anaitis

By the long arm of coincidence, then.

Jurgen

That's more appropriate—more dignified—as if I were

so small a thing as a finger.

Anaitis

I never, in all my incarnations, had such a Prince Consort. You talk so flippantly.

Jurgen

Nothing of the sort. Just because I am a little puzzled by your erotic dances, your weird sex practices, your shocking caresses—which I admit do you credit, nonetheless—and although I admire both your inventiveness and your industry—

Anaitis

You don't love me at all—and you mock religion. It's very disturbing.

Jurgen

But, darling—aren't you just the least, littlest, tiniest, very smallest trifle—bigoted?

Anaitis

How dare you?

Jurgen

Just because I lack your ardor in celebrating certain

tenets of your religion—no one admires these ceremonials more than I do—but I find the constant repetition of these ceremonials causing, shall we say, a lack of firmness in my responses. In short, darling, that is all there is to it.

Anaitis

Oh, never mind! I wish you would spend less time in the library and more time with me, that's all.

Jurgen

The library is the only place where I can avoid your guests.

Anaitis

It is necessary for one in my position to entertain, more or less. I can't close the door against my own relatives.

Jurgen

Such riffraff, though, my darling. I cannot congratulate you on your kindred. I do not get on at all well with people who are part man, part bull, or goat or what not. Priapos is the only fellow who comes here looking like a complete human being—and I had rather he stayed away, because even I am a bit envious of him.

Anaitis

And why, pray?

Jurgen

Well, while I go reasonably well equipped with Caliban, Priapos carries a lance I frankly envy.

Anaitis

It is a showy weapon, certainly—but not much use in actual combat.

Jurgen

My darling! And how do you know?

Anaitis

Why, Jurgen—how do women always know these things? By intuition, I suppose.

Jurgen

So! You admit you judge things by feeling them, rather than by reason. So be it! But, to get back to the congenial task of criticizing your kindred—your cousin Apis, for example is a good sort—but, say what you will, it is ill-advised for him to go about with a bull's head. It puts me out when I try to talk with him. So needlessly conspicuous.

Anaitis

But, I really must invite him.

Jurgen

Even so, my dear, in issuing invitations a hostess may fairly presuppose her guests will not make beasts of themselves. To come in such a zoologically muddled condition shows a certain lack of respect for you, my darling.

Anaitis

But, it's all in the family. Sometimes, I despair of your taking your proper place in the social life of Cockaigne.

Jurgen

But they have no conversation. I am driven to the verge of virtue by their imbecility. And as for your female relations—

Anaitis (instantly jealous)

Which of those sluts has been making up to you? Ishtar? Aphrodite?

Jurgen

Now, some of them are enticing enough.

Anaitis

I knew it! But you need not think you deluded me.

Jurgen

Be reasonable, darling. Cousin Io, for example, is incarnated as a heifer, Venus as a swan, and Thouieris as a hippopotamus. How can you reasonably be jealous of ladies with such taste in dress?

Anaitis

And I know perfectly well who it is! It is Diana, that Ephesian hussy! Very well—very well, indeed. I shall have a plain word or two with her at once. The sooner she gets herself and her big chest out of my house, the better. I shall be quite frank with her. And, as for you, Jurgen—

Jurgen

But, my dear Lisa—

Anaitis

Why do you call me Lisa? Lisa was never a name of mine in any of my incarnations.

Jurgen

Slip of the tongue, my pet—an involuntary, but natural

association of ideas. As for Diana of the Ephesians—she reminds me of a pine cone with that eruption of breasts all over her, I can assure you.

Anaitis

I'll just bet.

Jurgen

You have no cause to be jealous. Never was I interested in a woman with more or less than two breasts in my life. In fact, I was always more of a leg man. Anyway, you know my heart is ever faithful.

Anaitis

It is not your heart I am worrying over, Jurgen, for I believe you have none.

Jurgen

Now, that's not fair.

Anaitis

You have quite succeeded in worrying me to distraction, if that is any comfort to you. However, let us not talk of it. It is now absolutely imperative that I go to Armenia to take part in the mourning for Tammouz. People will not understand if I were absent from such an important orgy.

Jurgen (giving her a husbandly kiss)

Be off and attend to your religious duties, my dear. I will stay here in the library until you come back.

Anaitis

Double dealer! You're up to something.

Jurgen

My love, you appear positively unable to keep away from virtuous persons. But why bother about them? Why tire yourself proselytizing? You might be so much more agreeably employed. Tempting anchorites can hardly be fun. Be tolerant of all things. In spite of all Heaven's efforts, man's mingled nature is apt to develop a strain of respectability.

Anaitis (going)

You just have no religious sense.

Jurgen

Enjoy the orgy.

(Anaitis leaves in a huff.)

Jurgen

Well, well, even the pleasures of Cockaigne do not

entirely satisfy me. No, it is something else I desire—and Anaitis does not quite understand me. Her point of view is all very well—maybe death does end all things; yet if the outcome proved otherwise, how much more pleasant for all concerned to have established amicable relations with the overlords of the second life by doing whatever they expect of one here. And I do feel something is expected of me. Reason assures me that I am indispensable to the universe; but with reason somehow does not travel belief. I simply lack the credulity to be a free-thinking materialist. To believe that we know nothing assuredly, and cannot ever know anything with certainty—takes too much on faith. Therefore, I shall see to it that Jurgen does nothing which he cannot more or less plausibly excuse in the case of supernatural inquiries. That is far safer and only just. Why is it, then, I am not content? It seems to me there is some injustice being perpetrated on Jurgen, somewhere.

CURTAIN

ACT II
SCENE 7

Cockaigne, a few months later. Jurgen is talking to Anaitis.

Jurgen

And you say I have to leave?

Anaitis

The Master Philologist says so.

Jurgen

It seems as though I hardly got here.

Anaitis

I tried to talk him out of it, but he wouldn't listen.

Jurgen

Well, well, beyond doubt the situation is awkward. I was content enough in Cockaigne and it is unfair that I should be thus ousted. But, where will I go?

Anaitis

Into whatever land you may elect, dear. That much I was able to manage for you.

Jurgen

But I grow tired of all the countries I have ever seen. I have visited nearly all lands known to man.

Anaitis

That, too, has been arranged. You can go instead into one of the countries desired by men. Places never visited except in dreams.

Jurgen

How am I to choose without having seen them? It isn't fair.

Anaitis

Why, I will show them to you. (she holds a crystal ball for Jurgen) It is Time's own glass which was left in my keeping when Time went to sleep.

Jurgen (peering)

What place is this?

Anaitis

Atlantis. Now look again.

Jurgen

Hmmm. No different from Cockaigne, I'd say. Into no realm of endless pleasure will I ever venture again. Glorified brothel, that. I'd always expect to be raided by the police.

Anaitis

Here is Arcadia.

Jurgen

I don't relish living in the forest eating nuts.

Anaitis

Here is Leuke, where Queen Helen rules.

Jurgen

Well, it looks all right—if the local by-laws allow me a rational amount of comfort.

Anaitis

Discomfort you would have in full measure. For the heart of no man remains untroubled after he has once viewed Queen Helen and the matchless beauty that is hers. I will not help you to go into Leuke, for you would forget me once you have seen Queen Helen.

Jurgen

What nonsense you are talking, my darling. I'll wager she cannot hold a candle to you.

Anaitis (sadly)

See for yourself!

Jurgen (peering in, slyly)

But, certainly this is not the Helen whose beauty launched a thousand ships?

Anaitis

I assure you that it is—and it is she who rules Leuke—whither I do not intend that you shall go.

Jurgen

But, darling, this is preposterous. The woman is nothing to look twice at. To call her beautiful is exaggeration, and I must protest in simple justice.

Anaitis (brightening)

Do you really think so?

Jurgen

Most assuredly, my love. Do you remember what Calpurnius Bassus says about blondes?

Anaitis

No, I believe not. What did he say, dear?

Jurgen

I would spoil the splendid passage by quoting it inaccurately from memory. But he was right. His opinion is mine in every particular. An inferior kind of beauty. So, if Helen is the best Leuke can offer, I had best go somewhere else.

Anaitis

Oh! I see, some other little slut has taken your fancy.

Jurgen

There was a bull dancer in Atlantis—a tasty morsel by the look of her. Quite an acrobat, too. Now she might content me for a while. She resembled you, dear—that's why I like her—very close resemblance, except that she had a better figure. If I must part with you, I intend, in common fairness to myself, to find a companion as like you as possible. You understand, I can pretend it is you at first, then gradually, imperceptibly you will fade from my memory without my experiencing any intolerable anguish.

Anaitis

So, you're already hankering after those sluts! And you dare to say they are better looking than I am! And you tell me so to my face!

Jurgen

There's no deceiving a woman's intuition. Yes, I love that little dancer in Atlantis. Who can blame me? Such a gorgeous figure. Yes, I elect to go to Atlantis.

Anaitis

Do you so! Do you so!

Jurgen

If not Atlantis, then Arcadia. There was a little shepherdess I saw with a matchless bosom. Too good to be wasted on some filthy shepherd.

Anaitis

Where you go, my fine fellow, is a matter over which I have control.

Jurgen

Then, do the fair thing and send me some place I'll be

happy.

Anaitis

You are going to Leuke.

Jurgen

I absolutely refuse.

Anaitis

We'll see about that.

Jurgen

My love, do be reasonable! We both agreed Leuke was totally unsuitable. Why, there are no attractive women there.

Anaitis

It is for that reason that I am sending you there. (she waves her scepter and the scene changes) I, at least, will miss you. Farewell, Jurgen.

(Anaitis disappears behind the scenery.)

Jurgen

Thank you, darling. I appreciate your kindness—and I foresaw it. But, this little trick was for your own good—it would be painful if you allowed your jealousy to overcome your better nature.

(Chloris, a pretty hamadryad, comes up and stares at Jurgen.)

Jurgen

So, this is Leuke. (to the hamadryad) How might I come into the presence of Queen Helen.

Chloris

You may gaze at Queen Helen between the hours of four and six every day at her palace at Pseudopolis. The public is welcome.

Jurgen

And is the Queen as fair as people report?

Chloris

Men say that she excels all other women immeasurably.

Jurgen

And what do women say?

Chloris

Women say that she excels all other women to the same degree that her husband excels all other men.

Jurgen

Married? I was not told that. I suspect Anaitis may have seen a little deeper into my character than I expected, the bitch.

Chloris

I, for one, see nothing remarkable in Queen Helen's looks. Frankly, I think that a woman who has been so much talked about ought to be a bit more careful in the way she dresses.

Jurgen

And, who is the lucky fellow to whom the Queen is married? Another forgiving cuckold like Menaleus, I trust.

Chloris

Why, to shining Achilles, the son of Peleus.

Jurgen

You mean that big bruiser who killed Hector of Troy?

Chloris

The same.

Jurgen

I thought he himself was killed by Paris.

Chloris

So he was—but he caused so much of a fuss in Hades when he recalled her beauty that he started on a second quest for Helen. Then the gods gave Helen to Achilles because they said a man who has once beheld Queen Helen will never regain contentment. Personally, I dislike to think men are so foolish.

Jurgen

Men are not always rational—but then so many of their ancestresses are feminine.

Chloris

But, an ancestress is always feminine. Why, whatever are you talking about?

Jurgen

Why, Queen Helen.

Chloris

Quite so. Well, the gods desired tranquility, so they gave Helen to Achilles just to cool him down. You know when he starts howling, it frightens everyone. They also reasoned that Achilles, being such a brave champion, would keep her away from other men and thus stop the usual sort of trouble from starting all over again. The gods want no more Trojan Wars. So Achilles got her—though for my part, I shall never cease to wonder what he saw in her—no, not if I live to be a thousand.

Jurgen

Thank you, very much for your information, young lady. I must observe this monarch Achilles before the world is a day older. A King is all very well—but no husband wears a crown that prevents the affixation of other headgear. I'm sure he won't feel the decoration at all.

(Exit Jurgen. Chloris watches him leave.)

Chloris

Such a nice young man—but he talks so funny. Well, maybe someday I'll meet someone. It's no fun being a hamadryad and staying alone in the woods taking care of an old tree. Why couldn't I have been born a nymph? It isn't fair.

BLACKOUT

The lights go up almost immediately. Jurgen returns, looking dejected.

Chloris

Hello. Back again, so soon?

Jurgen (mournfully)

Yes, back again.

Chloris

Did you see the Queen?

Jurgen

Not exactly. I saw Achilles. Quite a man, that Achilles. He bends horseshoes with three fingers. Throws a spear right through an armored chariot.

Chloris

And what have you to say about Queen Helen?

Jurgen

Why, there is nothing more to say of any woman when she has such a husband. I admire Achilles, I envy Achilles—and in a word, I fear Achilles. And it is not fair that he should be a better man than I—but he is.

Chloris

But, is the Queen not the loveliest lady you have ever seen?

(Jurgen produces a mirror and motions Chloris to look.)

Chloris

Why, it is only a mirror. All I see is my face.

Jurgen

It is the answer to your question. Now, do you tell me your name, my dear, so that I may know who, in reality, is the loveliest of all the ladies that I have ever seen.

Chloris

My name is Chloris, the Hamadryad. And I look a fright today. You're a strangely impudent fellow.

Jurgen

Doubtless. It is hereditary. I am King Jurgen of Eubonia.

Chloris

Why did you leave your kingdom?

Jurgen

Why, I had heard exaggerated reports about the beauty of Queen Helen.

Chloris

Rumor, in such cases, is invariably untrustworthy. But, how does a King come to be traveling without any retainers—or even a sword—about him.

Jurgen

I am incognito—but I have a staff, my dear. I keep it concealed. (opening his robe) It suffices me.

Chloris

Certainly, it is large enough, in all conscience. You call yourself a King, but you carry the bludgeon of a highwayman, and I am afraid of it.

Jurgen

Presently, you will not be afraid of me or my staff.

Chloris

I think I hear someone coming.

Jurgen

Do not fear—I have my staff.

Chloris

Ah, you have great faith in that staff of yours.

Jurgen

I fear no man when I brandish it.

Chloris

But, others fear you?

Jurgen

Possibly. For I am Jurgen, and I deal fairly with all women, and raise my staff against none save in the way of kindness.

(Jurgen pulls her to him.)

BLACKOUT

The lights go up. Chloris is weeping.

Chloris

I think we should be married.

Jurgen

I already have two wives and it is only fair to confess it.

Chloris

But, you just got here today!

Jurgen

That is true.

Chloris

Then Jugatinus has not had time to marry you—and he would never marry you to two wives.

Jurgen

No. Jugatinus, whoever he is, didn't marry me on either occasion.

Chloris

So there. That settles it. Now you see for yourself.

Jurgen

To be sure, that does put a different light on it.

Chloris

It makes all the difference in the world.

Jurgen

I would hardly go that far.

Chloris

Why, you talk as if everybody did not know that Jugatinus marries people.

Jurgen

Be fair. I didn't say that.

Chloris

And as if everybody was not always married by Jugatinus.

Jurgen

Here in Leuke, but not outside of Leuke.

Chloris

But nobody leaves Leuke. I never heard such nonsense.

Jurgen

Still, the people of other countries do get married.

Chloris (patiently)

No, Jurgen. Jugatinus never leaves Leuke—so how can they?

Jurgen

Ah, but in Eubonia—

Chloris

Let's talk of something else. I do not blame you men of Eubonia—because men are all such swine—so they can't help it. Still, women ought to have the strength of character to keep out of such irregular relationships. So, do not let us talk about these persons you are so delicate as to describe as your wives. I appreciate your nobility, but let's drop it.

Jurgen

Still, in the absence of Jugatinus, might not someone else—

Chloris

Nonsense. Nobody but Jugatinus can really marry people. And so, no one else does.

Jurgen

What makes you so sure of that?

Chloris

Why, because nobody ever heard of such a thing.

Jurgen

That is an entire code of philosophy. Be that as it may. Let us, by all means, go to Jugatinus and be married. I yearn for respectability.

CURTAIN

ACT II
SCENE 8

Jurgen is lead in under guard by some soldiers. The Priest and the Queen of Philistia observe.

Priest

Lead in the prisoner.

(Jurgen is brought forward.)

Priest

You are an obsolete illusion. Now that we of Philistia have conquered Leuke, all such as you will be tossed in the ashcan of history and myth.

Jurgen (stoutly)

I am no illusion. I am flesh and blood—and besides, I am the high King of Eubonia. In disputing these facts you contest circumstances so well known hereabouts as to rank among mathematical certainties—and that makes you look foolish, as I tell you for your own good.

Priest (angrily)

We would have you know that we are not mathematicians—and we have no King in Philistia—where all must do what is expected of them.

Jurgen

How, then, can you be the leaders of Philistia?

Priest

Why, it is expected that women and priests should behave unaccountably. Therefore, all we who are women or priests, do what we will—and the men obey us. And it is we, the priests of Philistia, who do not think you can possibly have any flesh and blood under a shirt which we recognize to be a conventional figure of speech.

Jurgen

It is the shirt of Nessus.

Priest

It does not stand to reason. And certainly you could not ever prove such a thing by mathematics and to say so is nonsense.

Jurgen

But, I can prove it by mathematics. I can prove anything you require, by whatever means you prefer—for the simple reason that I am a monstrously clever fellow.

Queen (to the Priest)

I have studied mathematics. I will question this young man in privacy. You may go.

Priest (leaving)

Hail Queen Dolores, Empress of Philistia and the adjacent isles.

(Priest and guards exit.)

Queen

Now, you who claim to be flesh and blood—and King of Eubonia, too—what is this nonsense you were talking of proving by mathematics?

Jurgen

Well, but my mathematics are Praxagorean.

Queen

What! Do you mean? Praxagoras of Cos?

Jurgen

As if anybody had ever heard of any other Praxagoras.

Queen

But he belonged the to medical school of the Dogmatici and was particularly celebrated for his researches in anatomy. Was he a mathematician?

Jurgen

The two are not incongruous, Madame—as I would be delighted to demonstrate.

Queen

Oh, I think I have heard of this school—though I have never studied it.

Jurgen

Our school postulates that mathematics is best inculcated by a concrete example.

Queen

That sounds rather complicated.

Jurgen

It can lead to complications.

Queen

Come, then—sit next to me—and explain what you mean.

Jurgen

Why, Madame, by a concrete example, I mean one that is perceptible to the senses, such as sight—and touch.

Queen

Oh, oh—now I perceive what you mean by a concrete example. And grasping this—I understand that complications must arise from the choice of a wrong example.

Jurgen

Well, then, Madame, it is first necessary to implant in you—by the force of example—a lively sense of the whole science of Praxagorean mathematics.

Queen

I perceive your point. Go on. I want a penetrating demonstration. But, what is become of your concrete example?

Jurgen

It is ready for you, Madame.

Queen

Be prepared to reason deeply.

BLACKOUT

When the lights go up, Jurgen is with the Queen, who is dressing.

Queen

Certainly this Praxagorean system is fascinating. You must teach me the higher branches. We can arrange some compromise with the priests—that is always possible with the priests of Philistia. And, as for your hamadryad—I will attend to her myself.

Jurgen

No, I am ready enough, in all conscience, to compromise elsewhere; but to compromise with the forces of Philistia is the one thing I cannot do.

Queen

Do you mean that, King of Eubonia?

Jurgen

I mean it as I mean nothing else. You Philistines are in many ways an admirable people. In all ways you are formidable. So, I admire, I dread, I avoid, and, at the very last pinch—I defy. For you are not my people, and willy-nilly, my gorge rises against your laws as insane and abhorrent. Mind you though, I assert nothing. I cannot go so far as to say you are wrong—but still, at the same time! That is the way I feel about it. So I, who compromise with everything else, can make no compromise with Philistia.

Queen

What a pity! Very well, then.

(The Queen claps her hands. The Priest enters with several other priests.)

Priests

Hail, Dolores, Empress of Philistia.

Priest (to Jurgen)

You must be relegated to the limbo of your fathers—as was foretold in the prophecies—in order that the prophecies may be fulfilled. Now, it appears that the progenitors of this flesh and blood prisoner were of a different faith than the Greeks who inhabit Leuke—and his fathers foretold a limbo called Hell.

Jurgen (contemptuously)

It is little you know of the religions of Eubonia!

Priest

We have it written down in this great book—without blot or error.

Jurgen

Then, you will see that the King of Eubonia is the autocratic head of the Church and can alter all prophecies at will. Learned Golwais says so directly, and the judicious Stevegonius was forced to agree with him.

Priest

Two notorious heretics. It was settled once and for all by the Diet of Othmar.

Jurgen

Hmm. You haven't read them in the light of Vessler's commentaries. And that is why you underrate Golwais and Stevegonius.

Priest

Vessler is a heretic.

Jurgen

What!

Priest

I tell you, I have been roused to indignation by his Historia de bello Veneris.

Jurgen

You surprise me.

Priest

Shocked by his Pornoboscodidascolo.

Jurgen

I can hardly believe it, even so, you must grant—

Priest

And horrified by his Liber de immortalitate Mentulae.

Jurgen

Conceding that—still, at the same time—

Priest

And disgusted by his de Modo coeundi.

Jurgen

Nonetheless—

Priest

And shuddered at his unspeakable Erotopaegnion!

Jurgen

Still—you cannot deny—

Priest

And have read the confutation of Golwais by Zanchius, Faventius and Tomas Geaminus.

Jurgen

You are very exact, sir, but—

Priest

In short, I have read every book you can imagine.

Jurgen

Sir, I expose you. You are fabricating. You cite books which never existed, by authors who never existed, to refute a book by an author I myself fabricated. What do you say to that?

All Priests

TO HELL WITH YOU!

Jurgen

And I thought you were polite, reasonable men.

(Enter Chloris, led by a guard.)

Chloris

Farewell, Jurgen. I care nothing of what these priests of Philistia say about me. But woodsmen are felling my tree to make a bed for the Queen of Philistia.

Jurgen (to the Queen)

Is this true?

(The Queen smiles and nods.)

Priest

It is what the Queen ordered the first thing this morning.

Jurgen

You women! What man would ever have thought of that!

Chloris

When my tree is felled, I must depart to Hades and I must taste of Lethe and forget all I have loved.

Jurgen

You should give thanks to your forefathers that your fate is no worse. I am to be banished to Hell—a barbaric place where people are actually tortured for their sins. See the danger of having a morbid ancestry. Dear girl, so long as you remember me—do so with charity.

Chloris

Jurgen, you were never unkind. I have loved you well.

Jurgen

And I you. Not with a heroic love, nor with madness and high dreams—but with a love befitting my condition—a quiet, gentlemanly, middle-aged love.

Chloris

Jurgen, you have loved me as much as you were able. No matter, you are Jurgen, and I have loved you.

Priest

Lead them to their fates.

Queen

Reconsider, Jurgen.

Jurgen

Never.

Priest

To Hell with him!

CURTAIN

ACT III
SCENE 9

Hell. Several devils are torturing sinners. Enter Jurgen.

Devil

Now, who may you be that come to us still alive?

Jurgen

It would not be treating honestly with you to deny that I am the Emperor Jurgen.

Devil

But, we are rather overrun with Emperors and politicians. Their crimes are a great trouble to us. Were you a very wicked Prince?

Jurgen

Never since I became Emperor has one of my subjects uttered a complaint against me.

Devil

Either you cut out their tongues or you scared the Hell out of them, didn't you?

Second Devil

Your conscience then, does not demand that you be punished?

Jurgen

My conscience, gentlemen, is too well bred to insist on anything.

Devil (skeptically)

You don't even wish to be tortured?

Jurgen

Not at all. I had expected something of the sort— (brightly) But I will not make a point of it. In fact, I shall be quite satisfied without it.

Devil

Well, well, this is very fine. We like you. You must be the only unpretentious person in Hell. You wouldn't believe the self-conceit of most ghosts. Their demands are outrageous.

Jurgen

Really, I should hardly think that.

Devil

Why, we have to punish them until they are convinced that their sufferings are just and adequate. You have no notion what elaborate tortures some people insist on. Especially people with nice consciences. It quite tires us out.

Second Devil

What's a poor devil to do?

Jurgen

Why is this place called the Hell of my fathers?

Devil

Because your fathers built it in dreams.

Jurgen

Whatever for?

Devil

Out of the ridiculous notion that whatever they did on earth was of eternal importance. Pitiful self-conceit.

Jurgen

I quite agree. And all my forefathers are here, you say?

Devil

Only the ones with what is known as a conscience.

Jurgen

Then, I'm sure that I don't belong here.

Devil

Do you suppose you could persuade some of your relatives to go elsewhere? They are really a terrible nuisance.

Jurgen

I will try to obtain justice for you. Dispensing justice is my imperial duty. Let me talk to your leader.

Devil

Oh—you'll want to see Grandfather Satan.

Jurgen

I always prefer to deal directly with a principal.

(A devil passes by, beating an old man.)

Jurgen

Say, I know that old sinner from somewhere.

Devil

Him. He's the worst person here. There is absolutely no pleasing that man!

Jurgen

Nobody knows that better than I. Good day, Father.

Coth

Eh? Who are you that bids me good day? It is a terrible day. Can't you see that I'm suffering horribly, stupid?

Jurgen

Don't you know me, Dad?

Coth

How should I know you, when I never saw you before in my life? Is this kid stupid or what?

(The Devil beats the old man as they go off.)

Jurgen

Humph.

(Enter Grandfather Satan.)

Devil

Here comes Grandfather Satan now. You can talk to him.

Jurgen

What is the meaning of this insane country? There is no sense in it—and no fairness either.

Satan

Why, that is what I was telling my wife last night.

Jurgen

You have a wife, then? Why, that explains a lot. Either as a Christian or as a married man, I should have known that was your due. And how do you get on with her?

Satan

Pretty well, but she does not understand me.

Jurgen

Et tu, Brute.

Satan

Are you making some derogatory remark?

Jurgen

No, no. Just pondering the fate of all poor devils.

Satan

You have a complaint, I take it—about the accommodations? Well, in this hotel we don't take complaints. We can make it worse, but not better.

Jurgen

It is not as it was rumored to be in my capital at Breschau.

Satan

And where is that?

Jurgen

In Noumaria, where I am Emperor. You know where that is?

Satan

Of course, I have studied geography. You have to know everything in a job like this. And I've often heard of you—though never of your being Emperor.

Jurgen

This place is simply not in touch with new ideas.

Satan

It's the war with Heaven. It takes up too much of my time. In any event, what can I do for you, my distinguished guest?

Jurgen

I want to know how this hellish place was created.

Satan

It was done by Koschei—who makes things as they are—to humor the pride of your forefathers.

Jurgen

I think he might properly have humbled their pride.

Satan

No, no. Koschei will do almost anything to humor pride, for it is the one thing impossible to Koschei. And your forefathers were exceedingly boastful of their sins.

Jurgen

I should think Koschei would be very proud—making everything.

Satan

But there is nothing else, you see. How then can Koschei be proud?

Jurgen

Ah, I see. It's like listening to one's own poems.

Satan

Exactly. Or directing one's own play.

Jurgen

Well, I am of the firm opinion Koschei should never have given in to the impulse to make this place. However, since he did, you must assist me to leave it.

Satan

Why is that?

Jurgen

Because I am the Emperor Jurgen, that's why—and a monstrously clever fellow—and I don't care for this place.

Satan

I am sorry, but once you check in, you don't check out for a while.

Jurgen

How long must I stay?

Satan

I don't know. It depends entirely on what your father thinks about it.

Jurgen

Why, in that case I may never leave. But what has he to do with it?

Satan

Since everything here is here because of his absurd notions of guilt—as you so frequently have proved by logic. Everything. Even you.

Jurgen

Hum! I shall have to have a word with the old gentleman.

Satan

Meanwhile, you are my guest. Would you care to see your room. Delightful view of the inferno.

BLACKOUT

When the lights go up, Jurgen and Coth are arguing.

Coth

Now that I look at you, rascal, I can see very well that you are my son. Small wonder I meet you here. And how is it that a worthless creature like you became an Emperor?

Jurgen

Is this a place to talk about earthly dignities? I am surprised, sir, that your mind still runs on empty vanities.

Coth

Don't be sassy with me, you whippersnapper. Anyway, there is no justice in this place—and no way of getting justice.

Jurgen

But, Father, your crimes do not amount to very much.

Coth (raging)

Is that so? And what do you know? I killed eight men in cold blood.

Jurgen

But that was fifty years ago—and much more interesting things have happened since.

Coth

I broke the Sabbath many times.

Jurgen

Pooh!

Coth

I spoke disrespectfully to my mother!

Jurgen

Pish!

Coth

I committed adultery.

Jurgen

Well, that, at least, is more interesting to talk of—how

many times?

Coth

Seven. Seven times.

Jurgen

Is that all?

Coth

That's what your mother said.

Jurgen

A very perspicacious question. But what does it matter if you did all that and more?

Coth

Oh, go away. This is a torment beyond endurance to be plagued by silly questions. I demand you lazy devils apply more fuel. These coals are not hot enough.

Devil

We are doing the very best we can, Milord, but your tastes are very difficult to satisfy.

Coth

All I want is a little service.

Devil

Fuel is in very short supply. There is a war on.

Jurgen

Dad, I think you should be less demanding. After a man has been dead a little while, what does it matter what he did?

Coth

But, my conscience, my son—that is the point.

Jurgen

Why do you insist on restricting the conversation to matters I do not understand? After all, we haven't seen each other in many years and we might well talk a bit of pleasanter things. I appear to be here for an indefinite stay, so we can talk of your guilt another time.

Coth (primly)

Your presence is a comfort to me that my sins do not justify.

Jurgen

Why, do you actually care about me, one way or the other?

Coth (weeping)

You were an idle, rebellious young wastrel, but I loved you as a father must love his only son.

Jurgen

Hum. I never thought you did. And that may have had something to do with my rebelliousness—though I don't mean to excuse myself.

Coth

Don't worry. I'll never forgive you for it, you no good. All you ever had was excuses.

Jurgen

I wonder when you think I'll get out of here?

Coth

I have no idea.

Jurgen (coaxingly)

Yes, but what do you think?

Coth

You have a very uncivil habit of arguing with people.

Jurgen

Still, sir—

Coth

I have spoken to you about it many times—

Jurgen

That's true, but nonetheless—

Coth

I don't want to talk about it anymore.

Jurgen

And I say, that—

Coth (shouting)

When I say that I have no opinion—

Jurgen (shouting)

But everyone has an opinion, Father.

Coth

How dare you speak to me in that tone of voice!

Jurgen

I am fully grown and speak as I please.

Coth

Lord, what a torment. Why, this is worse than Hell!

Jurgen

Here's a pretty Father. Having imagined me in this place, you might at least imagine me out of it.

Coth

I can only think of your well merited affliction and of the host of light women with whom you have sinned.

Jurgen

Host, you say? Well, that's something. (slyly) Surely, there are no women here.

Coth

I think there are women here. It is reported that quite a number of women have consciences. But the women are kept separate for good reason. Your Mother would be meddling out of hand.

Jurgen (nettled)

Are you still finding fault with Mother?

Coth

She was, in many ways, an admirable woman, but she never understood me.

Jurgen

That was probably true. I understand how that could be. But still, I say this is nonsense about women being here.

Coth

It is not! How many times must I tell you that? And I want no more of your impudence.

Jurgen

I wager they are all ugly.

Coth

They are not! Why do you keep contradicting me?

Jurgen

Because you don't know what you're talking about. How could there be any women here? Is this a place for a lady? Besides, their flesh and bones would be cinders.

Coth

There are any number of vampires and succubae here. And they do not burn because the creatures are endowed with passions more hot than fire.

Jurgen

Indeed! Well, I must stay away from them.

Coth

You lie! I think you are on your way to meet a vampire even now.

Jurgen

What—a hideous vampire?

Coth

No, a seductive, beautiful, deadly vampire.

Jurgen

She can't be beautiful. You can't think that!

Coth

How dare you tell me what I think and do not think! I do think she is beautiful.

Jurgen

Well, I mean to have nothing to do with her.

Coth

I think you will. You will be up to your tricks with her immediately. Aren't you an Emperor—and aren't you my son? Come, Mr. Devil, beat me away—I can't bear to watch what is about to happen.

(The Devil beats Coth as they go off. Enter Florimel from the other direction.)

Jurgen

A good morning to you, Madame, and whither are you going?

Florimel

Why, no place particular—this is my vacation—with none of my ordinary annoyances to bother me.

Jurgen

And what could annoy so beautiful a vamp as you?

Florimel

Why, the trouble of seducing and murdering very naïve and likeable young men.

Jurgen

But, how did you happen to become a vampire if the profession does not pleas you? And what is your name, anyway?

Florimel

I'm Florimel. I used to be a flower girl. Florimel, the flower girl. But one day I fell ill and died. It could happen to anyone.

Jurgen

But most women who die don't become vamps, do they?

Florimel

Oh, it was such bad luck. I have a stupid, thrifty sister. It was all her fault and it isn't fair.

Jurgen

But, what happened?

Florimel

Oh, as my funeral was leaving the house, a cat jumped over my coffin. It would have been perfectly all right in the end—they caught the cat and were going to kill it. My sister wouldn't let them!

Jurgen

She must have loved the cat.

Florimel

Not a bit of it. Someone wanted to buy it because it was a good mouser. She was simply too cheap to forego the money.

Jurgen

Typical family relationships.

Florimel

So, of course, I became a vampire.

Jurgen

Yes, I see it was inevitable. Still, it hardly seems fair. I pity you, my dear.

Florimel (sobbing)

A nice girl like me. But, who are you?

Jurgen

I am Jurgen, Emperor of Noumaria, King of Eubonia, Prince of Cockaigne, and Duke of Logreus. I am incognito at the moment, but doubtless you've heard of me.

Florimel (patting her hair straight)

To be sure! Who would have expected to meet Your Highness here?

Jurgen

One says—Majesty—to an Emperor. A detail, of course, but protocol is protocol.

Florimel

Of course, Your Majesty—you will excuse my lack of breeding. I am only a poor flower girl.

Jurgen (graciously)

Think nothing of it. I will see that your vacation passes pleasantly. I intend to deal fairly with you. I must say, my father imagines things very satisfactorily at times.

BLACKOUT

When the lights go up, Jurgen is in conversation with a Devil.

Devil

So, you have married a vampire?

Jurgen

Yes, but not for long. She is only on a two week vacation—and that is as long as most good marriages last.

Devil

Why, we approve of marriage, Jurgen.

Jurgen

Approve of it?

Devil

Certainly. Is it not written:—It is better to marry than to burn—? Marriage is a truly unique torture, most often self-inflicted—and beyond anything we poor devils can manage.

Jurgen

I thought all marriages were made in Heaven.

Devil

In the past. But since the war broke out, we have taken the trade away from the enemy. You may marry here as much as you like.

Jurgen

I shall marry in haste and repent at leisure. But, can one divorce here?

Devil

Oh, no. That would be like a remission of punishment—something that is never allowed. We trafficked in divorce for a while, but practically everyone who obtained one promptly thanked Heaven—which was not what we had in mind.

Jurgen

What do you do in Hell when there is no longer any putting up with your wives?

Devil

We would prefer not to tell you, for it might get back to their ears.

Jurgen

Hmm! Hell is pretty much like any other place. I

wonder if my first wife, Dame Lisa, is hereabouts. I certainly wished her here often enough.

Devil

Your wife was a shrew and the sort who believes whatever she does is right?

Jurgen

Yes. That was kind of a mania with her.

Devil

Then, she can't possibly be here.

Jurgen

You tell me news which, if widely known, would lead many men into a deliberate course of vicious living.

Devil

People are saved by Faith. And who has more faith in herself—in her own infallibility—than a mean-tempered wife?

Jurgen

You mean my Empress, the formidable tempered Dame Lisa, is in heaven?

Devil

Where else? Plainly, your wife was the sort that can be tolerated only by angels.

Jurgen

Humph! Well, I must do the manly thing and find her.

Devil

But, if you find her, what will you do then?

Jurgen

That I don't know. But I must search for her. Public opinion insists it is my duty.

Devil

Well, if you must, then do so. But we are sorry to see such a monstrously clever fellow going to such a benighted country ruled by an Autocrat who was not duly elected by his people.

Jurgen

I never thought of God as being an elected post.

Devil

Unfortunately, neither did he.

CURTAIN

ACT III
SCENE 10

The Pearly Gates. The young Jurgen, a boy of about ten, sits at the gates as a door keeper. Jurgen enters.

Jurgen

A good day to you, my fine young fellow. What are you thinking of so intently?

Young Jurgen

Sir, I was pitying the poor damned.

Jurgen

Why, you must be Origen.

Young Jurgen

No, my name is Jurgen.

Jurgen

Hum! You do look familiar. Very possibly you speak

the truth.

Young Jurgen

I am Jurgen, son of Coth and Azra.

Jurgen

Ah, but so were the others.

Young Jurgen

I am Jurgen, the grandson of Steinvor—the one she loved above all her other grandchildren. So, I abide forever in Heaven with all the illusions of Steinvor. But, who are you, with the fine looking shirt?

Jurgen

I am Pope John the Twentieth, though I really ought not to tell you.

Young Jurgen

Let me look at the guest register. All Popes are admitted immediately without inquiry into their private affairs—to avoid any tincture of scandal. And we have twenty-three Pope Johns listed. Sure enough, the mansion for Pope John the Twentieth is vacant. He seems to be the only Pope not actually in Heaven.

Jurgen

Of course not. Can't you see I'm right here?

Young Jurgen (checking his computer)

None of the others in your series can place you. John the Nineteenth says he never heard of you.

Jurgen

How could he? He died before me. What a dolt I must have been at your age.

Young Jurgen

And John the Twenty-First says he thinks they lost count and there never was a Pope John the Twentieth. You must be an imposter.

Jurgen

Child, can't you even do simple arithmetic? How could there be a Twenty-First if there wasn't a Twentieth? And what becomes of the principle of papal infallibility if there was a mistake like that?

Young Jurgen (fumbling with his computer)

But, still—

Jurgen

Either this John the Twenty-First, who says there was no John the Twentieth, is lying or he is telling the truth. If he is lying, don't believe him. If he is telling the truth, then quite plainly there was never any Pope John the Twenty-First—and therefore, because I don't exist, neither does he—which is nonsense.

Young Jurgen

Yes, sir, it all sounds very logical.

Jurgen

Even did we grant his insane contention that he is nobody, then in accordance with the proposition that nobody lies in Heaven—nobody is lying, so therefore, I must be speaking the truth, and you must believe me. Q.E.D.

Young Jurgen

That makes a lot of sense. You reason exactly as I do.

Jurgen

Why, it's a mathematical certainty.

Young Jurgen

Well, I'm going to let you in.

Jurgen

Ah, if only Lisa could see me now. Is my Grandfather King Smoit here?

Young Jurgen

No, no. My Grandmother never imagined that either her husband or her lover would go to Heaven—so they didn't.

Jurgen

This is a circumstance which heartens me to hope one may find Justice here. Yet, I'd best avoid Grandma—her illusion of me is pretty far from reality.

CURTAIN

ACT III
SCENE 11

God's Throne. God is seated on high, surrounded by angels. Jurgen enters and stands, looking up.

Jurgen

I fear you—and, yes, I love you—and yet, I cannot believe. Why could you not let me believe when so many others believed? Why could you not let me have faith—for you gave me faith in nothing—not even in nothingness? It's not fair.

God

I was never your God, Jurgen.

Jurgen

Once—very long ago. I had faith in you once.

God

No, that boy is here with me. And there is nothing of

that boy in Jurgen the man.

Jurgen

God of my Grandmother! God of my childhood. Why is it I am denied a God? Why can I never find Justice?

God

Would you look for Justice in Heaven of all places?

Jurgen

No, I perceive it cannot be here.

God

You have looked to find your God without. Never even looking within to see what is truly worshipped by the thoughts of Jurgen.

Jurgen

Ah, at least he is a monstrously clever fellow.

God

Doubtless, I do not meet many clever people here. Your god had neither love nor hate—not even for his only worshipper.

Jurgen (after a moment)

That's true. But then, you are only the delusion of my Grandmother.

God

That also is true. She would be contented with no rational explanation of things. She was a real skeptic. She refused to believe in things as they are.

Jurgen

That's Granny, for sure.

God

For your Grandmother, things as they are were only temporary afflictions. And so, she demanded to be taken to Heaven when she died.

Jurgen

Just like her. Don't spare the horses. And so she came here.

God

No, there was no such place. And she wouldn't be persuaded—so they brought her to Koschei—and Koschei made Heaven for her, so that she would leave him in peace: for your Grandmother is a very persistent and garrulous woman. And so, Jurgen, Koschei created me at that time.

Jurgen

But, how did he do it? How could he juggle things around like that?

God

Don't ask me. I am but the illusion of an old woman and am totally ignorant of celestial mechanics and all that.

Jurgen

All of this to please a woman who was not even faithful to her husband!

God

Koschei will do almost anything to humor love—for love is impossible to Koschei.

Jurgen

I thought pride was impossible to Koschei.

God

What is pride?

Jurgen

But, why is love impossible to Koschei?

God

How should I know? I am only the illusion of an adulterous old woman.

Jurgen

Well, well. I certainly cannot presume to contradict you.

God

You have proven it often by logic.

Jurgen

Even now that we are face to face, I do not quite believe in you.

God

Who could expect a clever fellow who sees so clearly through the illusions of an old woman to do that?

Jurgen

I am glad that things are arranged now so believers will not be disappointed. It is only fair that the faith they had in you forced even Koschei to be reasonable. And though I cannot quite believe in you, I believe there was never any other deity who had such dear worshippers—for you were loved by those whom I loved dearly very long ago.

God

Who could have expected such a monstrously clever fellow to be so mawkish about the illusions of an old woman?

Jurgen

Perhaps, everything is true, in a way, even though it isn't. Now that wouldn't be a bad solution.

God (smiling and descending from his throne)

Well, I can't answer that. Now, if you'll excuse me, I have some Heavenly business to attend to.

Jurgen

Oh, no ceremony, no ceremony.

(As soon as God exits, with his angels, Jurgen seats himself on God's Throne.)

Jurgen

Well, you have been Duke, Prince, King, Emperor, and

Pope. Do such dignities content you? Not at all! What will you do now? Fretful Jurgen, you who always complained because you had not your desire. What now is your desire? This scepter and this throne avail me not. For I am Jurgen who seeks he knows not what. For hereabouts are none of my illusions—and I must now return to such illusions as are congenial. After all—one must believe in something. All that I see here, I envy and admire—but I don't believe a word of it. And therefore, with nothing here will I be satisfied. I am going to see the manager!

CURTAIN

ACT III
SCENE 12

The backstage area filled with old props. There is a sign that says "Office of the Manager," beneath which Koschei sits puzzling out his accounts. Enter Jurgen.

Koschei

You find me busy with stellar accounts—which appear to be in a fearful muddle, as usual. But, what can I do for you, Jurgen? For you, my friend who spoke a kind word for things as they are?

Jurgen

I have been thinking, Prince—

Koschei

And, why do you call me a Prince?

Jurgen

I do not know, sir. But I suspect that my quest is ended

and that you are Koschei the Deathless.

Koschei

Something of the sort. My real name no man has ever heard, so we need hardly mention it.

Jurgen

Precisely, Prince. But I have come to learn why you made things as they are.

Koschei

Why, how else could I make them? Could I make them as they are not?

Jurgen

But Justice, great Prince! Justice! It seems to me that things are not quite fair.

Koschei

But, friend, I have nothing to do with Justice. On the contrary, I am Koschei, who made things as they are.

Jurgen

Your reasoning, Prince, is unanswerable. I bow to it. I should have foreseen.

Koschei

Certainly, as clever a clap as you.

Jurgen

But, would you tell me then, what is this thing that I desire but cannot find in any realm man has known or dared to imagine?

Koschei

I am not a psychiatrist, Jurgen. I am afraid I cannot answer your question on the spur of the moment. The desires of man seem to be as multitudinous as they are inconstant. In short, I haven't the foggiest.

Jurgen

You mean even you don't know what I want?

Koschei

No, not the least notion. If you don't know your own mind it is a little thick for you to expect me to help out.

Jurgen

Still—

Koschei

I suspect if you get whatever it is you do want, you would be happy with it. I more or less fix things that way. So, why worry about it?

Jurgen

But, haven't you been guiding my footsteps on my recent pilgrimage?

Koschei

Why, I do remember meeting you with great pleasure, but I must confess I have had one or two other things to do. Don't look so dejected. The universe is a big place.

Jurgen (petulantly)

You are trying to spare my feelings. You can't mean you don't know and don't care about all I've been through!

Koschei

Something like that. But, do reflect: I wish I thought myself half so important as you think you are.

Jurgen (to himself)

This Koschei is not particularly intelligent. But, why should I expect Koschei to be intelligent?

Koschei

What are you muttering?

Jurgen

I was reflecting that it was not very intelligent of me to expect you, great Prince Koschei, to care about poor me.

Koschei

Oh, I see. Very astute.

Jurgen (aside)

Or to expect Koschei to be clever. This goes far toward explaining a lot of things. Cleverness is the most admirable trait—but cleverness is never at the top and never has been.

Koschei

What's that?

Jurgen

I was saying that my wife is not a model of cleverness and her society must be a burden to you by now.

Koschei

I am not accustomed to women. And I was willing to oblige a fellow rebel.

Jurgen

But I, Prince, have always conformed to the custom.

Koschei

Your lips conformed, but all the while, you made verses. And poetry is man's rebellion against what he is.

Jurgen

But, is it possible that Koschei, who made all things as they are, is a rebel?

Koschei

Let us say it is possible.

Jurgen

Well, be that as it may—I am no longer sure—I wish to put this delicately—that you obliged me by carrying off my wife.

Koschei

What! You want the plague of your life back again?

Jurgen

Well, I'm not absolutely sure. But, I'm rather used to her—to having her about.

Koschei

Come, friend. You were a poet of some merit. The trouble was that your wife did not understand you.

Jurgen

True, true. But it's not good for a man to live alone.

Koschei

I have the ideal wife for you.

(Koschei claps his hands. Guenevere enters.)

Jurgen

Guenevere. But even more beautiful than when I saw you last.

Koschei

She is Queen Guenevere, now. A bit more beautiful for

having suffered for love of Lancelot. There's nothing like the smell of another man or woman to make her attractive. But she will be your wife, if you will have her.

Jurgen

Do you remember me, Guenevere?

Guenevere

No.

Jurgen

Hum. It must be that I no longer look so young. We will pass over the unflattering explanation that you have simply forgotten the unforgettable Jurgen. (pause) It seems as though I never really loved any other woman, save Guenevere, for again you made me think myself a god. Queen Guenevere, when man recognized himself God's vicar on earth, it was to protect and glorify you. Beautiful and frail, you were half goddess and half child. I recognize the call of chivalry—and yet, I am not longer sure I am God's vicar upon earth—and somehow, I suspect God, if he had his druthers, would have selected a more competent representative. I dare not love you—yet I cannot help it.

Guenevere

Of course you cannot help it—for I am Guenevere.

Jurgen

Madame and Queen. Once there was a man who worshipped all women. They were to him of a sacred, sweet, intimidating beauty. Then was shown to him a woman whom he once had loved—just as she was—not as he believed her to be—the goddess was unveiled to display such mediocrity that he wondered he once had loved her. Then he began to suspect that all women are like their parents, no wiser, no more subtle, no more immaculate than the mother who begot them. Madame and Queen, it is not good for any man to suspect this.

Guenevere

Certainly it is not the conduct of a chivalrous man or a true poet. Farewell to you then, Jurgen, for I am leaving you forever. It was said that, in making me, God used both hands. Approaching me, men thought of God. What I willed was neither right nor wrong: it was divine. And it is I that am leaving you forever.

(Guenevere turns on her heel and leaves, affronted.)

Jurgen

It is a sorrowful thing that's happening.

Koschei (cheerfully)

Let's try again.

(Koschei claps his hands. Anaitis enters.)

Jurgen

Anaitis! I believe that I am actually blushing.

Anaitis

Come with me, Jurgen

Jurgen

Back to Cockaigne?

Anaitis

No. That is a small country cottage. You must see my palaces. In Babylon I have a palace where many abide with cords about them and burn incense while awaiting their fate. In Alexandria I have a palace wherein it is always night—and there folk seek for monstrous pleasures even at the price of instant death.

Koschei

She tempts rather nicely.

Jurgen

Sweetheart, your pictures are painted with the daydreams of inexperience You forget you are talking to a widely married man. I remember your ecstasies—

but these things—these overmastering frenzies you are talking about—I've never found the flesh whose touch roused insanity.

Anaitis

Ah, Jurgen, and I thought you were a real man.

Jurgen

I think I lack the imagination. To pretend that what my body does or endures is of importance seems rather silly nowadays. And so, love, be off with you.

Anaitis

Farewell to you then, Jurgen, for it is I who am leaving you forever. Live tepidly if you will. Henceforward you must—for I, and only I can awaken the desire that consumes a man entire—and so wastes nothing—even though I leave that favored man forever like burned ashes. Join with the greybeards and the eunuchs, then—for I am leaving you forever.

(Anaitis exits in a huff.)

Jurgen

It's a sorrowful thing that's happening—and a very unfair one to boot. Farewell, Queen Anaitis.

Koschei

You really are hard to please. One last chance.

(Koschei claps. Enter Helen of Troy. Helen looks like Dorothy la Désirée. Jurgen kneels and shields his face.)

Jurgen

Lady of my vision, now Troy's sons are all in Hades, fire has consumed the walls of Troy—and the years have forgotten her golden conquerors—and still, you bring woe on woe to hapless men. Now, you are within arms reach—now, when I am no longer fit to mate with your perfection. For we who are taxpayers, as well as immortal souls, must live by politic evasions; we fall insensibly to common sense as to a drug—and whatever is rebellious, and fine, and unreasonable—is dead past resurrection. No man living who has reached my years is anything but the lackey of prudence and half measures. (passionately) Yet, even now, I love more than all this world. What more can an old poet say? (dejectedly) For that reason, lady, I pray you begone—because your loveliness is unendurable (in anguish) and a taunt past bearing. Upon my tomb let it be carved—Queen Helen ruled this man while he remained worthy.—(pause) But that was long ago. (gathering courage) And so, farewell to you, Queen Helen. Your beauty has been to me as a robber that stripped my life of joy and sorrow. Because of you I have loved no woman. And so, farewell to you, Queen

Helen!

(Helen turns and leaves without a word.)

Jurgen

It is so unfair!

Koschei

Some people are rather hard to please.

Jurgen (recovering his aplomb)

In selecting a wife, sir, there are all sorts of considerations. I do not prefer matrimony, you conceive—but in the presence of those beauties, I twaddled like a schoolmaster. Decidedly, Lisa is right, I am no poet. However, when I last saw her, she seemed somewhat less outspoken.

Koschei

But, you conceive, she was under a very potent spell.

Jurgen

Prince, you produce the most charming of women—but forget you are displaying them to a man of forty and something.

Koschei

Does that make so great a difference?

Jurgen

Oh, in so many ways. As one gets on, one handles one's sword less creditably, and one does not carry so heavy a staff as one once flourished. He no longer practices mathematics, and no longer reasons deeply—in fact, it is a relief.

Koschei

I cannot believe that, with the flower of all womanhood before you, you prefer your termagant wife.

Jurgen

I am, as usual, undecided. Couldn't you let me see her for a bit?

(Koschei claps. Lisa enters.)

Koschei

Very well, but I warn you, the charm has worn off.

Lisa

So, you bastard, you tried to get rid of me! Why didn't you just have me murdered? Oh, no. Too easy. You had me carried off by a devil. You'll pay for this.

Jurgen

I think I will take her back, Prince.

Koschei (horrified)

Think it over carefully. Don't forget the poet you might have been—

Lisa (whirling on Koschei)

You, shut up!

Koschei

I beg your pardon.

Lisa

You heard what I said! Interfering in a family quarrel! Who do you think you are, anyway?

Koschei

I am Koschei the Deathless.

Lisa

A likely story! As if I believe that. Now, Jurgen, don't just stand there with your mouth open like a dead fish.

Did you hear him call me a termagant—now are you going to protect me from the insults this scum hurls at me, or are you just going to stand there like the big coward I know you are? I guess I know the answer to that! I have been patient with you a long time, Jurgen—but how you can expect me to stay with you, I don't know—you are enough to drive a person mad. So, you'd better get home, right now. If you don't come—well, never come again, that's all. There's plenty of men who find me very attractive. So there!

(Lisa flounces out.)

Koschei

You had better stay here. You won't get any sleep if you go home.

Jurgen

No. I'd better be going. She'll only be worse if I don't make things up with her. Thank you for the kind offer.

Koschei

I really find this hard to believe—and I made things as they are.

Jurgen

Well, if you were a married person, you might understand. She really isn't too bad, and besides, practically every marriage is like that.

Koschei

I really didn't give enough attention to marital relations when I was making things as they are.

Jurgen (wryly)

I have often thought that.

Koschei

You might as profitably oppose a hurricane as a wife. Yet, you want her back. Now I do not commend your wisdom—but your bravery I regard as astounding.

Jurgen (modestly)

I often wonder at it myself.

Koschei

I manage affairs as best I can—but they get in a fearful muddle sometimes, and while I am infallible—mistakes do occur. Next time, if there is a next time, I will give more attention to details of this nature.

Jurgen

Yes. It's details of this sort that muck up the whole scheme of things.

Koschei

One thing, before you go.

Jurgen

What is that?

Koschei

I am going to change things.

Jurgen

Eh?

Koschei

None of the things you remember since you met that monk on the road and put in a word for me, none of those things happened.

Jurgen

How can you manage that?

Koschei

That is my business. I am the author, so to speak, and I'm doing a bit of editing. And so, farewell to you, poor Jurgen, to whom nothing in particular has happened.

Jurgen

Is this Justice?

Koschei

No, but something infinitely more acceptable.

Jurgen

What's that?

Koschei

Peace of mind.

Jurgen

I think you are right. And so, I ask you but one more question. What pleasure do you get out of all this?

Koschei

I contemplate the spectacle with the appropriate emotion—have no fear. And so, goodbye.

(Enter Dorothy la Désirée as a Countess.)

Dorothy

May I speak to you a moment, Messire the pawn-broker?

Jurgen

Very willingly, Countess.

Dorothy

I though you might pass this way. You conceive it would not be fitting for Hetman Michael's wife to enter your filthy shop.

Jurgen

Hum!

Dorothy

My husband's birthday approaches and I wish to buy him a gift without troubling him for the money. How much, abominable usurer, can you advance me for this necklace?

Jurgen

Forty English pounds.

Dorothy

But, that is not a fraction of its worth.

Jurgen

If you care to sell it outright?

Dorothy

Old monster! You know I cannot do that. I could not explain it.

Jurgen

I could make you an imitation, so that you could veil any—sacrifices—that are made necessary by your affection.

Dorothy

I must have a hundred English pounds and not a penny less.

Jurgen

If Messire de Nerac could manage to visit me—I am sure we could manage this business without any annoyance to Hetman Michael.

Dorothy

Nerac will come then. And you may give him the money precisely as though it were for him.

Jurgen

Yes, I prefer that. An estimable young man. A pity his debts are so large. He lost so heavily at dice with the Cardinal last night.

Dorothy

He has promised me that—I mean, Master Inquisitive, that I take a considerable interest in that knight's welfare. He is a near cousin of mine. And that is all I mean!

Jurgen

Precisely, Madame—he will come tomorrow at my shop. I shall always be delighted to serve you. And I will deal fairly with you.

Dorothy (relieved)

That is all. I must get back. Merci.

(Dorothy leaves hurriedly.)

Jurgen

In effect, I am offering to pimp for her, because as she grows older she will need more and more money to hold her lovers. She is handsome still—but young men have no conscience about older mistresses. Well, I'd better get home. Nothing whatever has happened. (suddenly frightened) Good Lord, I promised Lisa to bring butter and I've forgotten it. Am I in for it!

(Jurgen rushes off, greatly concerned.)

CURTAIN

ABOUT THE AUTHOR

Frank J. Morlock has written and translated many plays since retiring from the legal profession in 1992. His translations have also appeared on Project Gutenberg, the Alexandre Dumas Père web page, Literature in the Age of Napoléon, Infinite Artistries.com, and Munsey's (formerly Blackmask). In 2006 he received an award from the North American Jules Verne Society for his translations of Verne's plays. He lives and works in México.

www.ingramcontent.com/pod-product-compliance
Lightning Source LLC
LaVergne TN
LVHW041620070426
835507LV00008B/363